FOOD FIGHT

Alex Latimer

For Lily and Isla—A.L.

OXFORD
UNIVERSITY PRESS

Oxford is a registered trademark
of Oxford University Press in the UK

Text and Illustrations © Alex Latimer 2023

First published in 2023

British Library Cataloguing
in Publication Data

Data available

ISBN: 978-0-19-278036-2 (paperback)

1 3 5 7 9 10 8 6 4 2

Printed in China

www.oup.com

Let me tell you a story.
A story about a little fruit and a little vegetable
and a forbidden friendship . . .

Grape and Mushroom
were best friends, but . . .

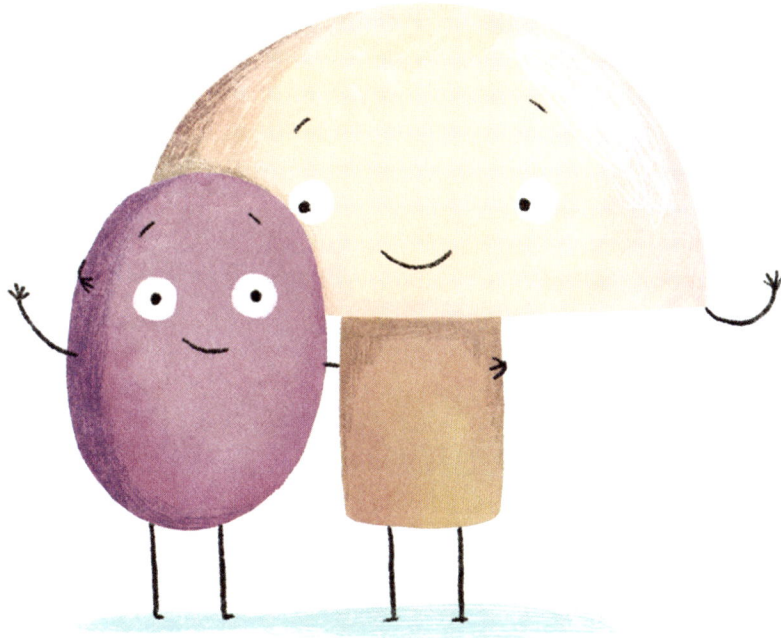

. . . they had a problem.

A BIG problem.

For as long as anyone could remember, the Fruits and the Vegetables had been fighting.

Keep your **MOULDY** mushroom away from our **GORGEOUS** Grape!

Your Grape is GROSS.
Our Mushroom is MAGNIFICENT!

And this made Grape and Mushroom very sad.

Lately things had become even worse.

First, Broccoli stole
Banana's skin . . .

. . . and left it just
where Orange
was jogging!

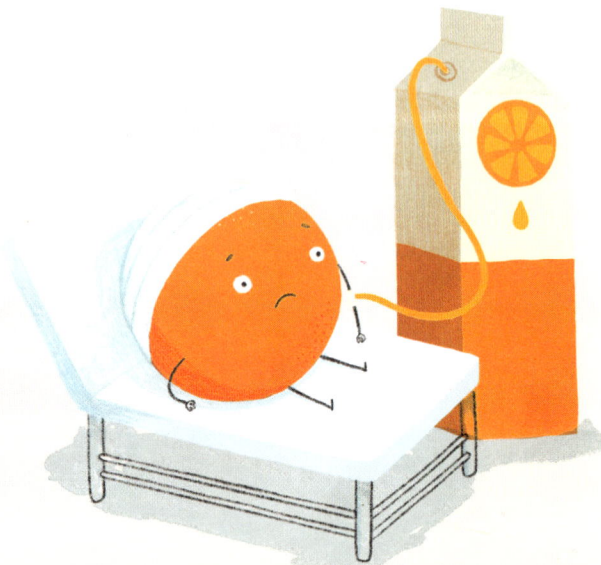

AAAH!

Then, to pay the Vegetables back, Apple and Pear found . . .

. . . the **masher** in the bottom drawer.

HELP!

No one could remember why they'd started fighting,
but the Vegetables thought of a lot of reasons to continue.

You fruits live in a
LOVELY BOWL
and we have to live
down in the bottom
of the fridge.

Have you ever
heard a mum say,
'If you don't finish your
FRUIT
you won't get
dessert? No!'

NO ONE likes Veggies.
We're always last on a plate.
Or scooped under the table
for the DOG!

And the Fruits found reasons to be bitter too.

You vegetables get to live in that cool white MANSION in the kitchen. The fruit bowl doesn't even have a roof. How is that FAIR?

Why do kids always take an apple for their teacher? How about a POTATO once in a while?

I'm telling you, if ONE MORE person picks me up and pretends to make a phone call, I'm going to go bananas!

But while everyone was fighting,
Grape and Mushroom snuck off to
play behind the coffee pot – in secret!

No one had ever seen The Wise Old Cheese.
Legend said that he lived on the Top Shelf of the fridge.
A place where no morsel had ever set foot, though many had tried.

So Grape
  and Mushroom
    packed their bags,

      trekked across
        the kitchen floor

        and crept
          into the fridge.

BUTTER

AQUA

They
climbed up
and up
and up.

KETCHU

They hiked through the blizzards
that blew in from the freezer,

and only just made it out of the spilt
yoghurt quicksand.

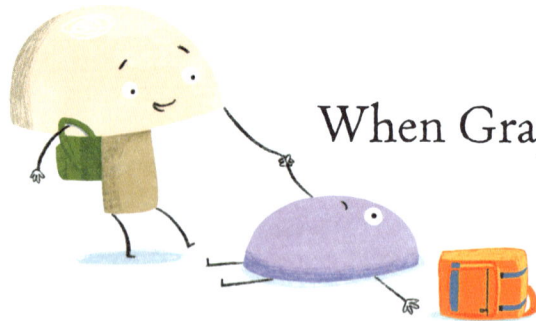

When Grape fell, Mushroom helped him up,

and when Mushroom said he couldn't go on,
Grape encouraged him.

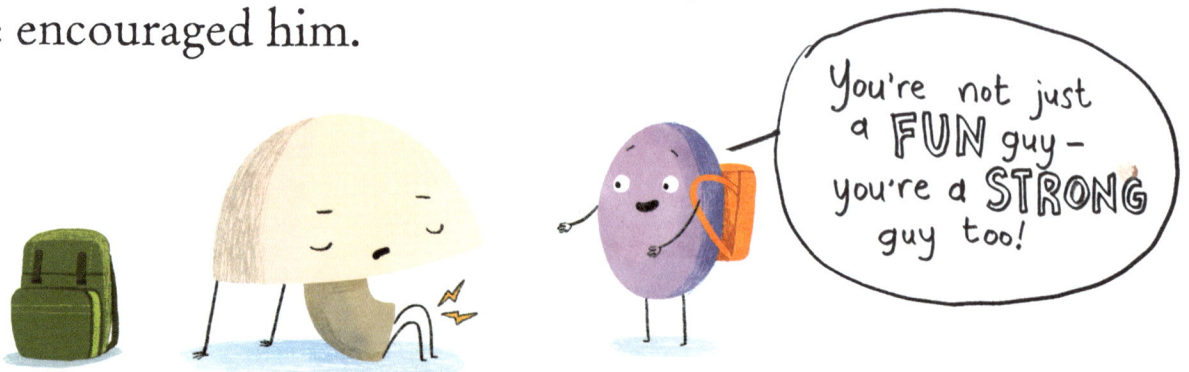

You're not just a FUN guy – you're a STRONG guy too!

They snuck behind
the Bad Eggs,

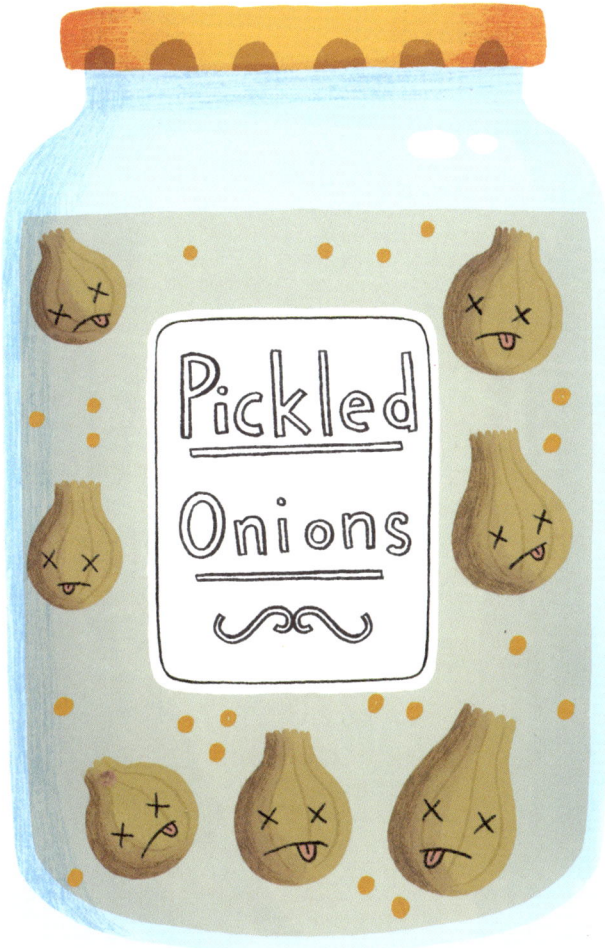

and on past things
that Fruits and Vegetables
should never see.

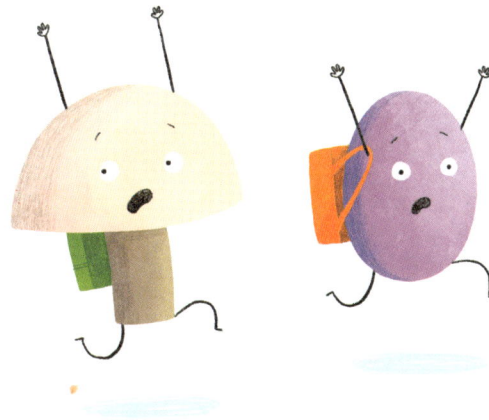

Until, finally,
exhausted, they reached . . .

There, surrounded by a mysterious light,
was The Wise Old Cheese.

He was very old.
Very smelly.
A little bit mouldy
and he had a
magnificent moustache!

Also, he was asleep.

'Oh, Great Cheese!' called Mushroom. 'There is no cheese greater! The Fruits and the Vegetables are fighting. They don't want us to be friends, but we're *best* friends. Only you, Oh, Great One, can make them stop.'

There was a grumble.
Then a whiff of old socks.

The Wise Old Cheese opened one beady eye and took a rasping breath.

'This is it,' Grape whispered to Mushroom.

'Let me think about it,' answered The Wise Old Cheese.

And, with that, he closed his eyes and and fell asleep again.

Is that it?

That was a bit rubbish!

When Grape and Mushroom arrived back, the Fruits and the Vegetables were STILL fighting.

Goodbye, my friend

Goodbye

I know CARRATE!

Grape and Mushroom parted ways, but . . .

. . . when they turned back for one final wave,
they saw something INCREDIBLE!

There was a mysterious milky light.

A familiar pungent pong.

The Fruits stopped their fisticuffs.

The Vegetables stopped

their squabbling.

They all stood still and

GASPED!

There, in front of them,
in all his mouldy glory, was . . .

. . . THE WISE OLD CHEESE!

He'd come to help after all!

'Fruits! Vegetables! I have come to put an end
to this fighting. These two tiny morsels made an
Epic Journey to the Top Shelf to seek my help.

No way!
No morsel has
EVER made it
to the
Top Shelf!

They came because they dreamed of a better world. A world where Fruits and Vegetables live together in harmony.

Imagine the things *you* could do if you all acted a bit more like these two friends.'

WOW! They got all the way to the Top Shelf? That is amazing!

And before long, the Vegetables and the Fruits realised something.

Can you believe Grape and Mushroom got to the Top Shelf? Not even I could do that.

Of course you could, Pear. If I helped you.

I've always loved your colours, Pineapple.

You seem sweet, Apple.

Oh, Onion, you're going to make me cry.

Something important.

I'm sorry about the masher, Potato.

I'm glad to see you're better, Orange.

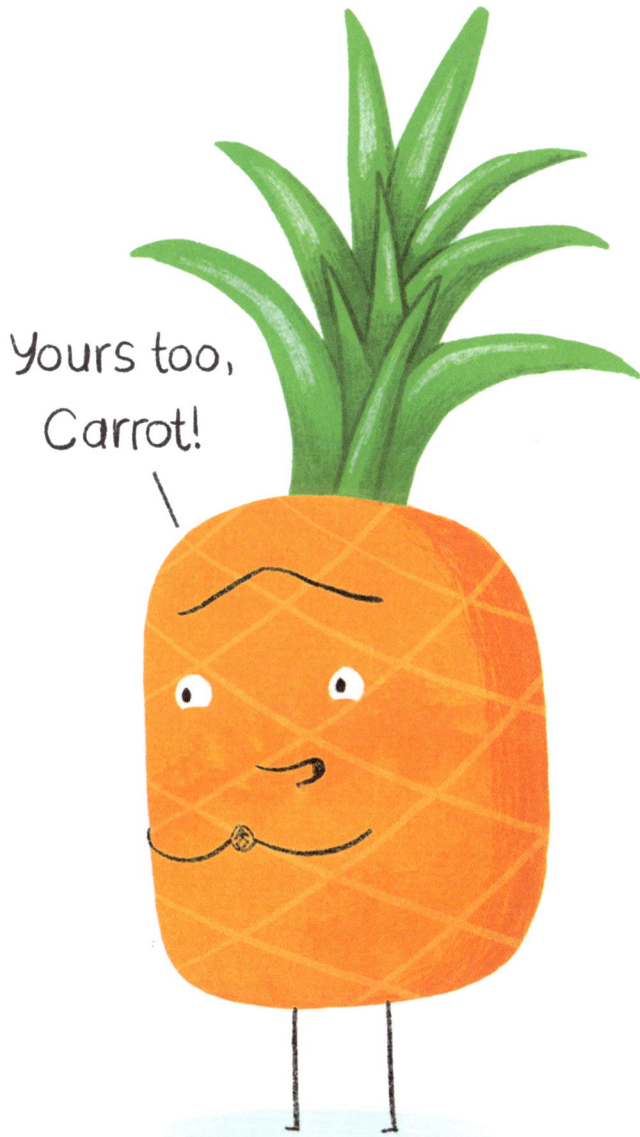

Yours too, Carrot!

Hey, Banana! You're in great shape!

You too, Courgette!

They realised that they actually had a LOT in common.

Perhaps The Cheese was right!

'Now we can be best friends again! Thank you, Wise Cheese,' said Mushroom. '*You* made them stop fighting.'

'No!' laughed The Wise Old Cheese. 'That was you guys. You showed them that Fruits and Vegetables can be friends. I just told them where to look.'

And with that, he was gone in a stinky yellow cloud.

Nowadays, the Fruits and the Vegetables get along really well, most of the time.

But when things get tense, there's an Old Mushroom and a shrivelled Grape with a story . . .

. . . of how a tiny fruit and a tiny vegetable, working together, made it all the way to the Top Shelf and brought the Fruits and the Vegetables together.

And me and my best friend, Grape here, climbed to the Top Shelf.

And we found The Wise Cheese and he WOULDN'T help us! So I said, listen up, buster . . .

And if there's ever a real emergency, they can still call on **The Wise Old Cheese.**

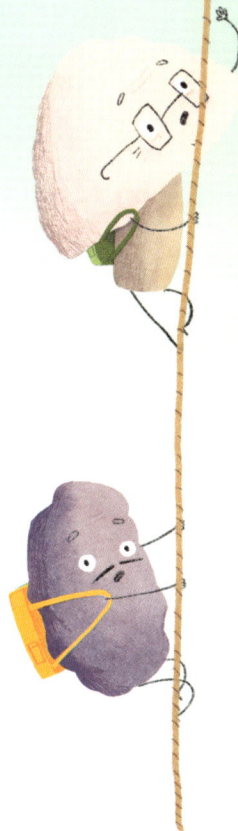

— Wise Old Cheese! We need your help **AGAIN!**

What is it THIS time?